Contents

		Page
1	Pay Up or Else	1
2	A Curse	4
3	Mathers Dies	7
4	A Bad Dream	9
5	Illness	12
6	The Doctor	15
7	A Good Rest	18
8	A Moth	20
9	All a Dream	23
10	The Bonfire	26

1

Pay Up or Else

'Please – give me more time,'
said the old man.
'I know I can get the money together.'

Jim Griggs smiled.
He was a large man with a friendly face.
'I'm a fair man,' said Jim Griggs.
'I don't want to make things
too hard for you.
I could give you a little more time to pay.'

'Oh – thank you!' said the old man.
'Just a few weeks . . .'

Jim Griggs shook his head.
'No, no – not a few weeks.
You see, the money is due today.
It must be paid today.
When I said a little more time, Mr Mathers,
I was thinking of a few hours.'

His smile had gone now.
He no longer looked friendly.
He looked as hard as nails.
'You see, we had an agreement.
I think people should stick to
their agreements.
So you'd better pay up. Or else.'

'But – I haven't got the money!'

'You should have thought of that
before you borrowed it.'

'I needed the money to keep the shop going!

I had no choice!'
Jim Griggs looked round the dark little shop.
There were books on magic.
Magic stones.
Magic wands.
Crystal balls.
Candles in the shapes of witches and demons.

A candle in the shape of a skull was alight.
It cast flickering shadows on the wall.
'Hardly worth keeping it going,' he said.
Still – if you sell the premises,
you'll be able
to pay me what you owe.'

He went to the door and turned round
the sign so that it said CLOSED.
'You'd better get in touch with
the estate agents,' he said.
'Put this place on the market.'

2

A Curse

'No, please – I beg you . . .' said Mr Mathers.

'You sell this place and pay me
what you owe!' shouted Jim Griggs.
He towered over old Mr Mathers.
'Or I'll send the boys round.
And you'll end up eating
hospital food for weeks.
And I'll *still* get the shop off you!'

'But if I sell the shop,
how am I going to make a living?'

'I don't know,' said Jim Griggs.

'And I don't care.
You should have thought of that
before you borrowed money from me.
If people will burn themselves –
well, that's not my problem.'

A moth flew in through the window.
'Look,' said Jim Griggs.
He pushed the candle towards the moth.
The moth flew into the flame,
and caught fire.

It fell to the ground, dead.

'You see?' said Jim Griggs.

'You play with fire, you get burned.'

'You'll be sorry for this,' said Mr Mathers.

'Not as sorry as you'll be,
if I don't get my money,' said Jim Griggs,
'I'm sending the boys round tomorrow.
The shop better be up for sale by then.'

'I'll put a curse on you,' said the old man.
'You think I don't know how?
Look at all these books.
They're full of spells.
I'll put a curse on you, I will.'

'Yeah, right, I'm really scared!'
Jim Griggs laughed loudly.
He was still laughing as he left the shop
and walked out into the night.

3

Mathers Dies

_____

Jim Griggs got his money, of course.
He always did.
Mr Mathers sold his shop
and Jim Griggs thought no more about it.
Until he went out to buy cigarettes
a few days later.
In the shop he caught sight of the local paper.
There was a photo of old Mathers.
'LOCAL MAN KILLS HIMSELF,' it said.
Old Mathers had cut his own throat.

His body was found
in a circle of burnt-out candles.

It must have been some strange ritual,
the paper said.
Perhaps it was to do with Hallowe'en.
Old Mathers was known for
his interest in witchcraft.
He used to keep an occult shop,
until it closed down.

Jim Griggs shrugged.
It wasn't his fault.
Silly old fool.
Why did he have to go and kill himself?

Tonight was Hallowe'en.
Not that Jim Griggs believed in
any of that rubbish.
He passed the common.
They were building a big bonfire there.
Chairs, tables, old rubbish –
it was piled as high as a house.
That'll make quite a blaze, thought Griggs.

4

A Bad Dream

Jim Griggs felt jumpy that evening.
It was a stormy night.
He heard the sound of kids outside,
doing trick-or-treat.
Once they knocked at his door,
but he didn't answer.
He heard the sound of
fireworks going off.

Jim Griggs poured himself a whisky,
and sat down to watch the television.
There was a horror film on.

An evil killer was
getting into people's dreams.
It made Jim Griggs feel even jumpier.
He switched it off and went to bed.

It took him a long time to get to sleep,
with the sound of fireworks outside.
When he did sleep, he had a bad dream.
A very bad dream . . .

Mr Mathers was standing by his bed.
His throat was all red
where he'd cut himself.

'Do you remember me, Griggs?' he said.
'I've put a curse on you.
It's a good curse.
You're going to turn into a moth.
And you're going to fly into a flame.
You're going to burn up, Griggs. Burn!'

Jim Griggs sat up with a start.
Just for a moment,
he thought he saw Mathers
still standing by the bed.
But it was just a bad dream.

His heart was beating fast.
It took him a long time to get back to sleep.

5

Illness

When Griggs woke up the next day,
he felt ill.
His throat was dry.
He had a headache.
He had a funny feeling,
like pins and needles,
in his arms and legs.

His hands felt clumsy,
as if they belonged to someone else.
When he was making tea,
the teapot slipped from his hands.
It smashed on the kitchen floor.

'What's wrong with me?'
Griggs asked himself.
He remembered his dream.
Mathers and the curse.
He didn't like thinking of it.
It gave him a nasty feeling.

He got into his car
and drove to his office.
He couldn't work today, though.
He couldn't keep his mind on the job.
He kept stopping what he was doing
and putting his head in his hands.

'Are you okay, boss?' asked Nick.
Nick was one of his boys.
'You look terrible.'
'I feel terrible,' said Griggs.
'You'd better go home,' said Nick.
'You can't work if you're ill.'
'No, better go home.' said Griggs.

'Go to the doctor,' said Nick.
'Yes,' said Griggs.
'Better phone the doctor.'

He got up from his desk with an effort.
and drove home very slowly.
He phoned the doctor and made an
appointment for the next day.

Then he lay down on his bed
and tried to sleep.
But every time he closed his eyes,
Mathers came into his mind.
Standing there with his throat all red.
'I've put a curse on you,' he was saying.
'You're going to burn up. Burn!'

Griggs felt hot. He was sweating.
He got up and ran to the bathroom.
He was violently sick.

6

The Doctor

Griggs drove to the doctor's
the next morning.

'What seems to be the trouble?'
asked the Doctor.

'I'm ill,' said Griggs.
'I feel funny. I feel tired.
I can't eat.'

The Doctor examined Griggs.
'I can't find anything wrong with you,'
she said.
'Are you under stress at work?'

'Not really,' said Griggs.
'I mean, I'm busy, but that's normal.'

'No personal problems?'

Griggs thought of Mathers and his curse.
That was stressful, all right.
But he couldn't tell the doctor that.
'No, no, I'm – I'm fine.'

'You probably just need to rest.
We all get run down.
Take a couple of days off work.'

'Thanks, doctor.
I will,' said Jim Griggs.

He hadn't taken a day off in ages.
Too busy making money.
Maybe a rest was just what he needed.

7

A Good Rest

Jim Griggs phoned the office.
He told Nick he wouldn't be in
until next week.
Then he tried to have a good rest.

It wasn't easy.
He felt tired,
but he couldn't sleep.
He felt hungry,
but he couldn't eat.

He kept thinking of Mathers and his curse.
Stupid old man!
Griggs wished he'd never met him.

Well, Mathers was dead now.
He couldn't do anything to hurt Griggs.
That was what Griggs told himself.
But late at night,
it wasn't so easy to believe.

Two days went by.
Still Griggs felt no better.
He looked in the mirror in the evening.
He hadn't shaved and his face looked furry.
His eyes looked big.
He looked like . . . a moth!
Don't be so stupid, he told himself.
His mind was playing tricks on him.
He'd be all right,
if only he could have a good rest.

He put himself to bed.
Worn out by the last three days, he was
asleep almost as soon as his eyes closed.

8

A Moth

The weak November sun
shone in through the window.
Griggs opened his eyes.
He felt funny.
He felt *different*.
He got out of bed.
Everything in his room seemed bigger.
The chairs were as high as his chest.
The door-knob was as high as his face.
It's me, thought Griggs.
I've – I've shrunk!

He put his hand to his head.

What are these things?
In a panic, he ran into the bathroom.
He looked in the mirror.
The face of a moth stared back at him.
Big eyes, furry face.
Two antennae growing out of his head.
Then he couldn't see himself
in the mirror any more.

He was getting smaller and smaller.
He looked down at his hands.
The fingers were fusing together.
His arms were turning into wings.
He was still getting smaller.
Shrinking down, down, down . . .

He tried to run from the bathroom,
but he couldn't run any more.
Suddenly he found he was flying,
from room to room in a blind panic.

In the kitchen, a candle stood on the table.
Griggs saw the yellow flickering flame.
It seemed to pull him towards it.
He heard Mathers' words again:
'You're going to fly into a flame.
You're going to burn up, Griggs. Burn.'
Then he flew straight into
the yellow heart of the flame.

9

All a Dream

Jim Griggs suddenly sat up in bed.
His eyes opened.
He was panting for breath.
His heart was beating fast.
He looked at his hands.
They were normal, thank God –
it had all been a dream.

Slowly, his heart returned to normal.
What a nightmare!
Thank God it was over now.
Jim Griggs realised he felt better.
He felt fine.

He didn't feel ill any more.
Maybe he'd needed that nightmare.
To sort of get rid of all his fears.
He was all right now. He was okay.

Outside, he heard
the sound of fireworks going off.
Today was November the fifth.
He looked out of the window.
It was dark.
He saw rockets blaze up in the night sky.
He must have slept all through the day!

He got dressed.
He felt like going for a walk.
Getting a bit of fresh air.

Fancy believing all that rubbish
about Mathers and his curse!
Fancy dreaming he'd turned into a moth!

It was funny, really,
when you thought about it.
Well, he'd been ill,
but he was better now.

He whistled as he walked out of the door.
He felt fine.
He decided to walk over to the common
and see the bonfire.

10

The Bonfire

The night air was cold on Jim Griggs's face.
He liked the feel of it.
He could see his breath in the air,
as if he was a dragon.

There was a crowd of people
on the common.
They were all standing around the bonfire.
Griggs could see its orange glow in the sky.

He suddenly felt happy.
All these people, gathered round
the bonfire to enjoy themselves.

That was a good thing.
Maybe he should start being nicer to people.
Go a bit easier on them . . .

He was close to the bonfire now.
He could see its bright sparks flying up.
Around the edges, the flames were red.
In the middle, where it was hottest,
they were bright yellow.

Griggs moved closer still,
pushing through the crowd.
Now he was right next to the fire.
He looked into its yellow, flickering heart.
It seemed to pull him towards it.

Suddenly, he heard Mathers' voice
in his head.
'You're going to burn up, Griggs. Burn!'
Griggs tried to hold back –
but he couldn't.

The pull was too strong.
'No!' he screamed.

He was still screaming
as he ran straight into
the yellow heart of the fire.